Original title:
The Dance of Dependability

Copyright © 2024 Swan Charm
All rights reserved.

Author: Eliora Lumiste
ISBN HARDBACK: 978-9916-86-605-4
ISBN PAPERBACK: 978-9916-86-606-1
ISBN EBOOK: 978-9916-86-607-8

The Trustworthy Waltz

In the dance of shared delight,
We move as one under the moonlight.
With every step, a promise made,
In shadows cast, our fears do fade.

Together we twirl through night's embrace,
In laughter's echo, we find our space.
With trust we weave this gentle thread,
In perfect rhythm, our hearts are led.

Harmony in Dependence

In the silence where our hearts align,
We find a strength that feels divine.
Like notes that sing in perfect tune,
Together we blaze beneath the moon.

Each heartbeat thrums a sacred bond,
In every challenge, we respond.
With gentle hands, we lift and rise,
In harmony, we reach the skies.

String of Certainty

A thread connects our souls so tight,
In moments shared, we find our light.
No doubt will break this steadfast line,
In unity, our hearts entwine.

Through storms and trials, we stand tall,
A tapestry woven, we shall not fall.
With faith as strong as the starlit sea,
The string of love binds you and me.

Ties that Bind

In every glance, a story told,
With hands clasped tight, we brave the cold.
The ties that bind are forged in grace,
In love's embrace, we find our place.

Through rivers deep and mountains high,
Together we soar, like birds on high.
With every laugh, our spirits climb,
In the tapestry of life, we rhyme.

The Gentle Push of Reliability

In the quiet of dawn we stand,
With steady hands, we shape our plans.
A whisper of faith in the air,
Soft as the heart that dares to care.

Through storms we sail, side by side,
Trusting the winds to be our guide.
Every step we take feels right,
A promise shines, a beacon of light.

Bridging Gaps with Timeless Trust

Across the chasm of uncertainty,
A bridge is built, a tapestry.
Each thread we weave, a tale of hope,
Together we learn how to cope.

Through laughter shared and secrets told,
In warm embraces, we feel bold.
Timeless trust, an anchor true,
In every moment, me and you.

Anchored in Each Other's Souls

In the depths where silence flows,
We find the strength that gently grows.
Anchored deep, our spirits thrive,
Together, we learn to survive.

When shadows loom and daylight fades,
In unity, no fear invades.
Two hearts entwined, we face the night,
With love's embrace, we reignite.

The Serenade of Safe Harbors

Underneath the starlit skies,
A melody of love softly sighs.
In safe harbors, our hearts reside,
Through every wave, we shall abide.

In laughter's tune and sorrow's song,
Side by side is where we belong.
Together, we weather the changing tide,
In the serenade of love, we confide.

Unseen Hands: A Holding

In the quiet of the night, it feels,
Gentle whispers, soft as light,
A touch that guides, a hand unseen,
Cradling dreams, where hope has been.

Through stormy seas and rugged trails,
Support echoes where silence prevails,
Together we rise, together we stand,
In the embrace of unseen hands.

Like roots entwined beneath the earth,
Each heart learns the measure of worth,
As we journey on this winding road,
With unseen hands, we share the load.

When shadows loom and doubts take flight,
A presence lingers, steady and right,
In the dance of life, we find our way,
With unseen hands, we will not sway.

So hold on tight when the world feels cold,
For love surrounds in stories untold,
In every heartbeat, a promise lands,
Together we thrive, with unseen hands.

Graceful Steps of Certainty

On pathways lined with morning dew,
Each step we take feels fresh and new,
With purpose clear, our spirits glow,
In graceful steps, through ebb and flow.

With every turn, our hearts unite,
In harmony, we find the light,
In laughter shared, in dreams aligned,
Graceful steps, in love entwined.

Through winding roads and open skies,
We face the dawn, with hopeful eyes,
No fear in soul, no doubt to weigh,
With graceful steps, we find our way.

The rhythm of life, a gentle sway,
Together we dance, come what may,
In every moment, meaning grows,
Graceful steps lead where the heart knows.

So let us move with trust so deep,
In every promise that we keep,
With courage found, and dreams set free,
Graceful steps of certainty.

The Pulse of Cooperative Spirits

In every heart, a rhythm beats,
A harmony where kindness greets,
We gather round, our voices blend,
The pulse of spirits, hand in hand.

Together we forge, together we dream,
In community's light, we are a team,
With open hearts and minds so wide,
The pulse of life, we do not hide.

Through trials faced and joys we share,
In every moment, we show we care,
Cooperative spirits, strong and true,
In unity's embrace, we break through.

So let the world hear our song,
In solidarity, we all belong,
With every heartbeat, our goal in sight,
The pulse of spirits, soaring light.

As we journey forth, we make a pact,
To lift each other when plans distract,
In every step, we'll raise our cheer,
The pulse of cooperative spirits clear.

Ephemeral Touches of Trust

A fleeting glance, a soft embrace,
In moments brief, we find our place,
The air is thick with something sweet,
Ephemeral touches, where hearts meet.

A whispered word, a fleeting smile,
In passing time, we bridge the miles,
With trust in shadows, soft and light,
Ephemeral touches, pure delight.

The clock ticks on, yet here we stand,
In subtle gestures, life is planned,
Each fleeting moment, a delicate dance,
Ephemeral touches, a fleeting chance.

So treasure now, these passing hours,
In every heartbeat, beauty flowers,
For in the briefest, we can see,
Ephemeral touches set us free.

With open hearts, we let time flow,
In trust, we find what we both know,
In the fleeting, there's joy and fuss,
Ephemeral touches, a timeless trust.

Shadows of Loyal Footfalls

In twilight's glow, they softly tread,
Echoes whisper, stories spread.
Beneath the moon, their paths align,
Hearts entwined, a bond divine.

Through forests deep, and rivers wide,
Their loyal steps, side by side.
In shadows cast, their dreams ignite,
Together facing darkest night.

With gentle hands, they clear the way,
In every moment, they choose to stay.
Through trials faced, their spirits soar,
Loyal footfalls, forever more.

In laughter shared, in silence felt,
In every heartbeat, love is built.
Time's fleeting touch cannot erase,
The shadows dance, their warm embrace.

Through every storm, they bravely walk,
In whispered dreams, they softly talk.
Well-worn paths, a story told,
In loyal footfalls, hearts of gold.

Melody of Intertwined Paths

Like rivers winding under skies,
Two souls unite, where journey lies.
In every note, a tale is spun,
Melodies rise as one by one.

Through valleys low and mountains high,
Their music breathes, a soft lullaby.
In harmony, their spirits dance,
With every step, they seize the chance.

In whispers sweet and laughter bright,
They weave a song that feels so right.
Each note a promise, each chord a leap,
In intertwined paths, the love runs deep.

Through seasons change, their hearts remain,
In every joy, in every pain.
A rhythm forged, unbreakable bind,
In melody's embrace, they find.

In twilight's glow, the stars above,
Sing softly of their endless love.
The music lingers, pure and true,
A melody shared, just me and you.

Embrace of Trusting Souls

In quiet moments, hearts unfold,
Two trusting souls, a tale retold.
With gentle eyes that mirror grace,
In embrace warm, they find their place.

With every breath, unspoken prayer,
Together they rise, a sacred pair.
In silence shared, their fears abate,
Trusting souls, they celebrate.

Through stormy days and sunlit years,
They're woven tight through joy and tears.
In every glance, a promise made,
In embrace of trust, fears do fade.

In laughter's ring and softest sigh,
They find their wings, they learn to fly.
With every touch, the world fades away,
Trusting souls, come what may.

Their journey blooms, a vibrant scroll,
In the embrace of trusting souls.
Together forging life's great art,
Two trusting souls, one beating heart.

Harmonious Threads of Connection

In a tapestry woven fine,
Threads of connection, hearts entwine.
With colors bright and textures bold,
Stories of life and love unfold.

Through laughter shared and sorrows bold,
In every thread, a tale retold.
In whispered dreams, they stitch and mend,
Creating a bond that will not bend.

Each moment spun, a vibrant hue,
Harmonious threads, me and you.
In easy grace, their spirits blend,
Through every twist, around the bend.

In shadows cast and sunlight's grace,
They find their rhythm, find their place.
A circle formed, forever true,
Harmonious threads, our love's debut.

Through every trial, together strong,
In this rich pattern, they belong.
With every breath, their hearts ignite,
Harmonious threads, strength and light.

Steps Under Stars

Beneath the night sky wide,
We wander hand in hand,
Each step a soft glide,
In silence we understand.

The stars whisper low,
Guiding our gentle walk,
In shadows we grow,
Together we talk.

Moonlight paints our path,
With dreams yet to weave,
In each other's laugh,
We find what we believe.

A universe so vast,
Yet here we find grace,
The moments we cast,
In love's warm embrace.

Forever in this dance,
With footsteps aligned,
Under stars we prance,
Our hearts intertwined.

Footfalls of Commitment

In the still of the night,
We make our promises clear,
With every heartbeat's light,
We hold each other near.

Through trials and delight,
We walk our chosen road,
In each embrace, a rite,
Easing the heavy load.

The world may try to sway,
But our bond is so strong,
In each word we say,
We know where we belong.

With every footfall shared,
Our journey marks its course,
In knowing we have dared,
Love is our driving force.

We'll weather every storm,
With trust our guiding star,
In each other's warm,
We find who we are.

The Solid Framework

Each brick laid with care,
A trust that won't decay,
Together we'll prepare,
To face each brand new day.

With laughter as our glue,
And dreams as our design,
In every vision true,
Our hearts and minds align.

Foundations built on trust,
In storms we'll stand so tall,
Resilience is a must,
Together we won't fall.

A structure born of love,
Embracing all we've sought,
With guidance from above,
In lessons that we've taught.

In this solid embrace,
We lift each other high,
In our sacred space,
Together we can fly.

Ripple Effects of Kindred Spirits

Two hearts connect in gentle grace,
With every glance, we find our place.
Like ripples spread on stillest pond,
In kinship's bond, we grow so fond.

The laughter shared, a symphony,
In quiet moments, harmony.
With every gesture, every sigh,
In kindred souls, we learn to fly.

Though distance may try to pull apart,
The strings of fate connect the heart.
In each embrace, a world we weave,
In simple truths, we dare believe.

The path we tread, forever shared,
In every joy, we've both declared.
Together we rise, like sunlit rays,
Kindred spirits lighting our days.

Impressions of Enduring Trust

In shadows that whisper soft,
Where secrets softly weave,
The roots of trust grow deep,
In hearts that truly believe.

With every dawn that breaks,
Promises renew their shine,
A bond that never shakes,
Like stars that always align.

Through storms that fiercely roar,
We stand with steadfast grace,
Finding strength in the core,
Of love that time cannot erase.

In silence, hands held tight,
We glimpse the spirit's dance,
Guided by inner light,
In fate's unyielding chance.

These memories, a treasure,
In every heart they dwell,
They hold a priceless measure,
Of trust and love's sweet spell.

The Comfort of Shared Journeys

Along the winding road,
We share our tales and dreams,
In laughter's soft abode,
Life flows in gentle streams.

With every step we take,
Two souls blend into one,
In moments we create,
Our hearts beat like the sun.

Through valleys dark and wide,
Together we find light,
In unity, we bide,
Our spirits taking flight.

The map of life unfolds,
With each twist, we adapt,
In stories yet untold,
Our friendship is the pact.

In the glow of twilight,
As stars begin to gleam,
We walk without a fright,
In the comfort of a dream.

Pillars of Everlasting Assurance

Like ancient stones that stand,
We weather every storm,
Together hand in hand,
In hearts, we keep each warm.

Through trials fierce and bold,
Our faith will never wane,
In each other's hold,
We find our strength again.

With kindness, we define,
The essence of our ties,
In love's gentle design,
We rise to touch the skies.

Through whispers of the past,
We build a future bright,
In trust that's meant to last,
Our dreams take form in light.

So let the world unfold,
With all its wild allure,
In every heart, we hold,
A promise, pure and sure.

Steady Souls on a Common Path

In twilight's warm embrace,
We walk where shadows blend,
Each step, a silent grace,
With every twist, a friend.

Through fields of green we roam,
With laughter in the air,
Our hearts have found a home,
In moments that we share.

We climb the hills of hope,
With courage intertwined,
In unity, we cope,
As dreams are redefined.

With hands held firm and tight,
Our burdens seem to fade,
In love's unyielding light,
We find the strength we've made.

So side by side, we stand,
Through life's vast, winding paths,
With unwavering command,
Together, we will last.

Flow of Fidelity

In rivers deep, our vows do flow,
Through currents swift, our love will grow.
With every wave, our hearts entwine,
In shades of trust, your hand in mine.

Through storms that break, we hold our ground,
In whispered bonds, true peace is found.
As stars align to guide our way,
Together strong, we'll face the day.

In gentle tides, our spirits blend,
A timeless dance that will not end.
Each glance, a promise, soft and sweet,
United always, two hearts in beat.

With every turn, our story's spun,
In shared moments, we are one.
Fidelity flows, a river wide,
In its embrace, we shall abide.

Melodies of Assurance

In softest tones, our dreams align,
A symphony that feels divine.
With every note, a story flows,
In harmony, our courage grows.

The vibrant beats, they lift our hearts,
In perfect time, we play our parts.
With whispered love, the world will hear,
A melody that draws us near.

In every chord, a promise lives,
Through trials faced, our strength it gives.
The music plays, it guides our way,
With each refrain, we choose to stay.

As twilight falls, the stars ignite,
Together, we embrace the night.
With every song, our spirits soar,
In melodies, we find our core.

Trust's Embrace

In quiet moments, trust is sown,
A bond so strong, it is our own.
With open hearts, we share our fears,
In trust's embrace, we dry our tears.

Through shadows cast by doubt's cruel hand,
We stand together, firm we stand.
With every vow, we build a space,
A sanctuary, trust's warm embrace.

The path is clear, though storms may roar,
We face the trials, seeking more.
With every step, our faith will guide,
In trust's embrace, we shall abide.

Our souls entwined, a gentle glow,
In love's embrace, together grow.
Through every trial, hand in hand,
In trust we flourish, strong we stand.

Farewell to Fickle Prefaces

Words unspoken linger air,
A chapter ends, yet love lays bare.
In whispered tones, we say goodbye,
To fleeting moments, watch them fly.

Pages turn, but scars remain,
In stories lost, we feel the pain.
Fickle hearts, in masquerade,
Too easily, they love, then fade.

Yet in the silence, lessons dwell,
In every rise, in every fell.
We learn to cherish what is true,
And bid farewell, we craft anew.

With heavy hearts, we part the line,
What once was ours, will be divine.
For in the echoes of the past,
We find the peace that's meant to last.

Intertwined Paths of Promised Safety

Two souls walk down a winding road,
In whispered truths, our hearts bestowed.
With every step, a vow we share,
In tangled roots, we find our care.

The sun may set, the shadows grow,
Yet hand in hand, love's light will glow.
Through every trial, we stand as one,
In woven paths, we've just begun.

A gentle breeze, a calming guide,
In each other's gaze, we find our pride.
Amid the storms, we seek the calm,
Our destiny wrapped in serenity's balm.

The journey's long, but heartbeats sound,
With every turn, new joys are found.
In laughter and tears, we navigate,
Together we stand, our love innate.

Echoes of Encouragement

Through valleys loud and wide,
Your voice my steady guide,
Encouragement beside,
With you I can confide.

When shadows loom so near,
Your words light up the way,
In every whispered cheer,
You chase my fears away.

With every feat I gain,
Your faith fuels my ascent,
In joy and also pain,
Your heart is my content.

Together we will stand,
In triumph or in fall,
With kindness, lend a hand,
We rise above it all.

In echoes that resound,
Your spirit lifts my soul,
In love we are found,
Together we are whole.

Tidal Waves of Lasting Devotion

In shadows cast by moonlit dreams,
Hearts collide like roaring streams.
With every crash, our love resounds,
Eternal tides where hope abounds.

Together we stand, unyielding and strong,
In the tempest's heart, where we belong.
The thunder rolls, yet we remain,
Bound by the promise, free from pain.

Through crashing waves, we ride the storm,
In love's embrace, we find our form.
The ocean's call, a siren's song,
In its depths, we both belong.

As tides retreat, our spirits soar,
A bond that's true, forevermore.
No storm can tear what we've entwined,
Through life's wild seas, our souls aligned.

Footprints in Faith

Through sandy shores, our footprints trace,
In faith we walk, a steadfast pace.
With every step upon this ground,
In shared goals, our hearts are bound.

The waves may crash, the winds may blow,
Yet forward still, we choose to go.
With every challenge, we rise high,
In faith we trust, we cannot fly.

The journey long, the road unsure,
But hand in hand, we shall endure.
In footprints deep, our love will guide,
Together, still, we walk with pride.

As dawn unfolds, new paths appear,
With faith as light, we conquer fear.
Each step we take, a promise made,
In footprints of faith, never delayed.

Whispers of Unyielding Trust

In shadows deep, a promise made,
Whispers soft like dreams conveyed.
Through storms we stand, hand in hand,
In silence strong, we understand.

With every sigh, a secret shared,
In tangled paths, we have dared.
Beneath the stars, our hopes take flight,
Together we blaze through the night.

A bond that time cannot erode,
In trust, we find our shared abode.
No fears can shake what we've built true,
Each heartbeat echoes, me and you.

In twilight's glow, we softly tread,
Unyielding trust beneath our tread.
Through trials faced, we rise anew,
In whispers low, our hearts break through.

Tapestry of Reliance

Threads of gold and hues so bright,
We weave our dreams with pure delight.
Each nod of faith, a stitch so fine,
Together strong, our hearts align.

Patterns formed with every tear,
In the fabric, our souls are bare.
With laughter shared, our stories blend,
In every loop, a heart to mend.

Time may fray and shadows loom,
Yet in this weave, love finds its room.
With hands entwined, we face the storm,
In this tapestry, we stay warm.

Together we rise, a radiant hue,
In reliance born, our spirits grew.
With every twist, our truths unwind,
In this creation, peace we find.

Echoes of Steadfast Hearts

Whispers linger in the air,
Steadfast hearts, a bond so rare.
In every echo, love resounds,
In silent vows, our strength abounds.

Through trials faced and paths unknown,
Our steadfast hearts have softly grown.
With every moment shared in grace,
In truth and light, we find our place.

In shadows cast, we find our glow,
With every step, we learn and grow.
Together we dance in life's embrace,
Through every heartbeat, love we trace.

The years may pass, yet still we stand,
In echoes strong, we make our strand.
With steadfast hearts, we claim our claim,
In this sweet journey, love the name.

The Solid Ground Beneath Our Feet

In quiet strength, we find our way,
Roots intertwine, where we will stay.
Through storms that rage and trials deep,
The solid ground, our promises keep.

With every step, we build our trust,
In weary nights, it's hope we adjust.
Together we rise, with hearts entwined,
The solid ground, our dreams aligned.

The earth may tremble, but we will stand,
Hand in hand, we understand.
In laughter shared, in sorrows faced,
The solid ground, our truths embraced.

Beneath our feet, love's power grows,
In every challenge, together we chose.
A journey rich, a life complete,
On solid ground, our hearts repeat.

Together We Rise Through Seasons

With each new dawn, we greet the day,
Together we rise, come what may.
In springtime blooms, our spirits soar,
Through summer's heat, we crave for more.

Autumn leaves, they twist and turn,
In winter's chill, our hearts still burn.
Through every phase, our bond expands,
Together we rise, through shifting sands.

With laughter loud and quiet tears,
We've come so far, faced all our fears.
In every season, you are my light,
Together we rise, hearts shining bright.

Though paths may twist, and skies may gray,
We hold each other, come what may.
With hands so warm, we'll face the test,
Together we rise, our love expressed.

Balancing Act of Fidelity

On a tightrope, we walk so fine,
A balancing act, our hearts align.
With every step, we carry weight,
In gentle trust, we navigate fate.

Through tempests fierce, we hold on tight,
In twilight's glow, we share the light.
Through thick and thin, our promise stays,
The balancing act, love's endless praise.

With honesty, we weave our threads,
In every word, love's spirit spreads.
In laughter shared, and whispers low,
The balancing act, in life's great show.

Each misstep teaches, each fall reforms,
In perfect harmony, our love adorns.
Together always, we take the leap,
The balancing act, our hearts to keep.

The Tides of Timeless Alliances

Like ocean waves that ebb and flow,
Our bonds remain, forever grow.
Through sunlit days and stormy nights,
The tides of time, our love ignites.

In whispered winds, we hear the call,
In unity's strength, we shall not fall.
With every shift, our hearts align,
The tides of trust, a bond divine.

Through trials faced, we won't retreat,
The tides will turn, but not defeat.
In patience learned, we find our way,
The tides of time, lead us to stay.

With open arms and spirits free,
In timeless alliances, we are meant to be.
Each moment shared, in silence vast,
The tides of love, forever cast.

Rhythms of Reliability

In shadows cast by worries low,
Together we rise, together we go.
In every beat, our hearts align,
In the pulse of time, our dreams entwine.

With steady hands, we pave the way,
In storms of doubt, we choose to stay.
Each promise kept, a guiding star,
Through trials faced, we've come so far.

With whispered words, we share our fears,
In joyful times, we shed our tears.
A loyal friend, a steadfast light,
In darkest hours, you make me bright.

Through changing tides, our spirits soar,
In every heartbeat, we want more.
The rhythms beat, we move as one,
In this dance of trust, we've just begun.

The bonds we forge, the paths we take,
In every step, our fears will shake.
A melody sweet in harmony,
In love and faith, we find our key.

In Step with Trust

Along the path, our footsteps blend,
Each silent vow, a timeless friend.
In every glance, a promise made,
In shadows deep, our fears will fade.

The gentle sway of hands held tight,
In laughter shared, we chase the light.
Through ebb and flow, we find our grace,
Each moment shared, a warm embrace.

With open hearts, we share our dreams,
In whispered hopes, our spirit beams.
Together strong, we face the day,
In step with trust, we find our way.

The rhythm of our lives entwined,
In every challenge, we are kind.
With every trial that we face,
In unity, we find our place.

Through storms that rise, we stand as one,
In shadows cast, we see the sun.
Woven together, our hearts will sing,
In step with trust, our spirits bring.

Choreography of Support

In every turn, our steps align,
A dance of faith, a love divine.
Through lead and follow, we create,
In perfect time, we cultivate.

With open arms, we catch each fall,
In every stumble, we stand tall.
With gentle cues, we guide the way,
In this choreography, we play.

Through rhythm clear, we find our beat,
Each boundless heart, our love complete.
The dance floor wide, no room for doubt,
In every step, we scream and shout.

With every turn, our spirits rise,
In every move, a sweet surprise.
Together we flourish, side by side,
In this dance of life, we confide.

With beats that echo all around,
In unity, our hearts are bound.
With strength and love, support will flow,
In this choreography, we'll grow.

Woven Bonds

In threads of gold, our lives are spun,
Each moment shared, a journey begun.
Through laughter bright and shadows long,
In woven bonds, we find our song.

A tapestry rich, with colors bold,
In every thread, a story told.
With hands entwined, we face the storm,
In woven bonds, we keep each warm.

Through silent nights and sunny days,
In countless ways, our hearts amaze.
With every stitch, a deeper trust,
In woven bonds, it's a must.

We share the burdens, lift the veil,
In unity strong, we will prevail.
With every knot, our dreams take flight,
In woven bonds, we find our light.

Through scars and smiles, we carry on,
In woven bonds, we are not alone.
Each thread a promise, strong and true,
In this woven world, it's me and you.

Lattice of Lifelines

In the weave of dreams we stand,
Threads of fate in gentle hand.
Each connection, strong and bright,
Guiding us through day and night.

Through trials faced, we find our way,
Supporting each, come what may.
In the lattice, love does grow,
Binding hearts with every glow.

Moments shared, both great and small,
Together we rise, we shall not fall.
In laughter's ring and sorrow's sigh,
Our lifelines dance, and never die.

As time unwinds its silent thread,
In every heart, our stories spread.
We are the stitches, bold and fine,
In this tapestry, you are mine.

So let us cherish, day by day,
This lattice, where we find our way.
Hand in hand, we face the sun,
In this world, we are as one.

Embrace of Security

In the shelter of your arms,
I find solace, free from harms.
A warm cocoon, where fears subside,
In this embrace, I safely hide.

Like a fortress strong and true,
Where the world fades, just me and you.
In whispered dreams, we drift away,
To a place where hearts can play.

The worries melt like morning dew,
In this haven made for two.
Each heartbeat echoes love's refrain,
In this embrace, there's no more pain.

Through storms that batter, skies so grey,
I find my peace in your ballet.
A rhythm shared, we dance in time,
In each moment, life feels sublime.

So let the world spin wild and fast,
Within your arms, I'm free at last.
With every breath, I hold you near,
In this embrace, there is no fear.

Steps in the Same Rhythm

Together we walk, side by side,
In the dance of life, our hearts abide.
With every step, our spirits soar,
In sync we move, forevermore.

Each stride we take, a silent song,
In harmony where we belong.
Through winding paths and open spaces,
In every glance, love's warm traces.

In laughter shared and tears we shed,
Each step we take, the past we've tread.
A cadence soft, like gentle rain,
In every rhythm, joy and pain.

With hands entwined, we face the night,
Finding solace in the light.
As stars align and dreams ignite,
We journey forth, hearts burning bright.

So let us dance through thick and thin,
In every loss, in every win.
For in this life, our tales are spun,
In each step, we become as one.

Reflections of Resilience

In the mirror of time, we see,
Echoes of what used to be.
The scars we bear, a badge of fight,
In every challenge, we find light.

Like rivers flowing, strong and deep,
We rise again from each lost leap.
Through storms that test and winds that sway,
Our spirits soar, come what may.

With every bruise, we learn to stand,
In adversity, we take our hand.
A journey marked with strength and grace,
Through every trial, we find our place.

Resilience blooms like wildflowers,
In darkest nights, it seeks the hours.
With hearts entwined, together we grow,
In every setback, our courage shows.

So let us celebrate each scar,
A testament to how we are.
In life's reflections, bold and bright,
We dance on, embracing the fight.

The Steady Beat

In the heart, a rhythm flows,
Like the wind that softly blows.
A pulse that binds us, strong and true,
In harmony, just me and you.

With every beat, we feel alive,
Through highs and lows, we learn to thrive.
Together dancing through the night,
Our steady beat, our shared delight.

In shadows cast, love finds its way,
Guiding us through night and day.
Each moment cherished, held so dear,
The steady beat, what we revere.

Through trials faced, we stand as one,
With every heartbeat, battles won.
In silence shared, in laughter bright,
The steady beat, our shared light.

So let us march, hand in hand,
In this rhythm, we understand.
The music of our hearts entwined,
The steady beat, forever kind.

Bridges Built on Trust

Over waters deep and wide,
Bridges stand against the tide.
Crafted strong with care and love,
Built on trust, like stars above.

Each stepping stone, a promise made,
Through every storm, we won't evade.
Together crossing paths anew,
Bridges built, I trust in you.

With every beam, a story told,
Of hearts united, brave and bold.
In every gap, we find a way,
Bridges built, come what may.

Resilient through the tests of time,
Hand in hand, our spirits climb.
With trust as bond, we won't divide,
Bridges built, side by side.

In the distance, visions gleam,
A future bright, a common dream.
With every step, our souls align,
Bridges built, forever shine.

Trust's Gentle Whisper

In quiet moments, trust will speak,
A gentle voice when hearts are weak.
It tells us truths we long to hear,
Trust's gentle whisper, calm and clear.

Through trials faced, it guides the way,
A steady hand in disarray.
No louder sound, no grander call,
Trust's gentle whisper, we stand tall.

In shadows where doubts often creep,
This whispered promise, ours to keep.
A bond unbroken, love will bloom,
Trust's gentle whisper, dispels the gloom.

With every heartache, every tear,
The softest whisper draws us near.
In silence found, in moments brave,
Trust's gentle whisper, our hearts save.

So let it guide us through the strife,
The tender thread that weaves our life.
In faith and hope, we shall bask,
Trust's gentle whisper, all we ask.

Steps of United Purpose

With every step, our goals align,
In the march of time, a shared design.
Through challenges faced, hand in hand,
Steps of united purpose, we stand.

In unison, our voices rise,
A chorus sung beneath the skies.
Each stride we take, a choice to make,
Steps of united purpose, no mistake.

Together forging paths anew,
With courage strong, we push on through.
For every dream, a shared embrace,
Steps of united purpose, our grace.

In moments fraught, we anchor down,
As one we rise, no need to drown.
Strength in numbers, hearts united,
Steps of united purpose, ignited.

So let us journey, side by side,
With hope and trust as our true guide.
In every step, with visions bright,
Steps of united purpose, our light.

The Symmetry of Reliability

In the quiet hours of dawn,
Trust stands tall like a tree.
With roots that burrow deep,
It sways softly in the breeze.

Promises etched in time,
Whispers in the shadows fall.
Each assurance builds a bridge,
That weaves us through it all.

When clouds gather overhead,
And uncertainty takes its course,
The pillars of our bond,
Remain steadfast, a powerful force.

In laughter and in sorrow,
We find a shared refrain.
Together we weather storms,
With faith that won't wane.

Through seasons that come and go,
A testament to trust we weave.
The symmetry of our hearts,
Is what we truly believe.

Murmurs of Enduring Allegiance

In the silence of the night,
Soft whispers dance on air.
A vow that binds us close,
In shadows, we declare.

With every heartbeat syncing,
An echo of our truth.
Endurance in each glance,
A bond that feels like youth.

Through trials we've encountered,
Our voices blend as one.
In every fleeting moment,
Our loyalty weighs a ton.

The journey may be long,
With valleys, peaks in view.
Yet hand in hand we march,
Our spirits ever true.

Amidst the swirling chaos,
In patience, we invest.
Murmurs of allegiance,
In our hearts, they rest.

Flowing Together as One

Like rivers merge and twist,
Two currents blend in grace.
Guided by the same moon,
We find our rightful place.

In harmony we travel,
With dreams that intertwine.
The paths we choose together,
A tapestry divine.

With every step we wander,
Our shadows dance in light.
The whispers of the journey,
Bring warmth to every night.

Through torrents and through calm,
Our spirits have been spun.
Flowing like the water,
Together, we are one.

In laughter and in silence,
The world fades from our view.
No distance can divide us,
For love remains the glue.

The Bonded Journey of Two

Two hearts set on a quest,
With dreams like stars aligned.
Every challenge a test,
In each, the love we find.

Through valleys dark and deep,
We climb the steepest climbs.
Hand in hand, no fear,
Our rhythm sounds in chimes.

A dialogue unspoken,
In glances, we convey.
Each moment shared is golden,
In the light of every day.

With every laugh and tear,
We stitch our tale anew.
The bond we share is strong,
A journey made for two.

As seasons turn to memories,
We sit beneath the sky.
In love, we've found our place,
A bond that will not die.

Echoing Cadences of Certainty

In shadows cast, a whisper flows,
Each thought a lantern, softly glows.
With every heartbeat, clarity,
Revealing truths, a symphony.

In silent nights, the echoes call,
A gentle guide that doesn't fall.
Through winding paths where doubts may roam,
The steadfast pulse will lead us home.

From whispered doubts to roaring faith,
Through storms of life, we find our wraith.
Resonant voices, strong and clear,
In certainty, we persevere.

The tapestry of dreams entwined,
In every note, our hearts aligned.
A cadence born from deep within,
In echoes, strength, we find our kin.

With every step, our spirits soar,
In harmony, we yearn for more.
The chime of hope, a vibrant song,
In cadence, we forever belong.

Weaving the Threads of Togetherness

In gentle hands, a loom of care,
Threads of laughter weave through air.
A tapestry of every soul,
Each knot a story, making whole.

Through sunny days and rainy nights,
We bind our hearts with shared delights.
In every strand, a memory,
Creating bonds that set us free.

With colors bright, we stitch our dreams,
In life's grand canvas, hope redeems.
Together strong, we face the tide,
In unity, we will abide.

As moments pass and seasons shift,
In every thread, a cherished gift.
Weaving tales of joy and strife,
In togetherness, we find our life.

A circle formed, no end in sight,
In woven hearts, we find our light.
For every thread, a silent vow,
In love's embrace, we take a bow.

The Harmonious Soliloquy of Support

In whispered tones, a soothing sound,
Where hearts entwined in trust are found.
A soliloquy both soft and strong,
In unity, we sing our song.

With open arms and steady hearts,
In every word, compassion starts.
Through trials faced, we stand and fight,
In harmony, we find our light.

Each note a pledge, no one alone,
In strength shared out, love's undertone.
A melody that heals our past,
In support's embrace, we hold steadfast.

From gentle whispers to thunder's roar,
In every struggle, we want more.
With courage found and spirits high,
Together, we reach for the sky.

In the symphony of hearts we blend,
With every note, a helping hand.
The harmonies of life resound,
In support's grace, true love is found.

United Steps Through Time

In every glance, the past reflects,
Moments frozen, heart connects.
Together through the sands we stride,
In memories where we confide.

Through winding paths and roads less trod,
With every leap, we beat the odds.
Though time may flow like rivers wide,
In unity, we shall abide.

Each step a story, every laugh,
In all we share, the photograph.
As seasons change and years unfold,
In every chapter, we're consoled.

With hands held tight through storm and shine,
Our footprints carved, our hearts entwined.
In the journey long, we find a way,
Through timeless steps, we choose to stay.

With memories cherished, futures bright,
In every dawn, we chart the light.
United still, through thick and thin,
In love's embrace, our lives begin.

Shaping Tomorrow with Steadfastness

With every step we take, we mold,
A vision bright, a story told.
Hands together, strong we rise,
In unity, we touch the skies.

Through trials faced, we stand our ground,
In steadfast hearts, our strength is found.
Though shadows fall, we'll light the way,
For brighter tomorrows, come what may.

With patience sown like seeds in earth,
We craft a world of endless worth.
Together, bold with hope in sight,
We shape the dawn, igniting light.

Our dreams like rivers, flow and bend,
Creating paths that never end.
We set the course, we chart the tide,
In every heartbeat, dreams abide.

So let us stand, both firm and true,
For shaping tomorrow starts with you.
With steadfastness, we take our flight,
Through boundless skies, we'll claim our right.

Illuminated Understanding in Each Step

Each footfall echoes wisdom's grace,
In quiet moments, we find our place.
Through journeys taken, lessons unfold,
In understanding, hearts turn gold.

With every stumble, we learn to grow,
Illuminated paths begin to show.
In shared reflections, we gain our sight,
A tapestry woven, day and night.

Each question asked, a bridge we build,
In the spaces shared, our souls are filled.
Through struggles faced, we find the light,
Connecting hearts with insights bright.

In gentle whispers, truth takes flight,
Guiding us forward, toward what's right.
Together walking, hand in hand,
With illuminated minds, we stand.

So let each step be filled with grace,
In every heartbeat, love we trace.
Illumined paths we choose to roam,
In understanding, we find our home.

Fabric of Friendship: Sewn in Trust

Threads of laughter, woven tight,
In fabric bright, our hearts take flight.
With every stitch, we mark our vows,
A bond unbroken, here, and now.

Through changing seasons, we stand fast,
In friendship's weave, a love that lasts.
With open arms, we share our views,
In trust, we find the strength to choose.

When shadows loom, we light the way,
With threads of hope, we chase dismay.
In every heart, a story spun,
Together bright, we shine as one.

Embracing flaws, imperfections lend,
A depth to love that will not bend.
With each new day, our colors blend,
In fabric rich, our hearts transcend.

So here's to bonds that time can't fray,
In friendship's arms, we'll always stay.
With trust as our foundation stone,
A tapestry of love we've grown.

Resilient Hearts Amidst the Storm

When thunder roars and tempests rise,
Resilient hearts will not disguise.
Through darkest nights, we stand as one,
In every trial, our strength begun.

With heavy winds that bend the trees,
Together, we find courage to seize.
In stormy seas, we raise our sail,
Through crashing waves, we will prevail.

The lightning flashes, bold and bright,
Yet in the chaos, shines our light.
Each heartbeat strong, we stand our ground,
In unity, our hope is found.

Amidst the struggles, hands we hold,
To share our stories, fierce and bold.
With love entwined, we weather all,
In every storm, together we call.

So fear not trials that come our way,
For resilient hearts will always stay.
Through raging storms, we'll rise and soar,
In unity, forever more.

Pages of Togetherness

In the quiet corners of our days,
We write our stories, in gentle ways.
Each word a promise, soft and true,
Binding our hearts, me and you.

Through laughter shared and tears we shed,
In every chapter, love is spread.
Turning the pages, hand in hand,
Together we flourish, together we stand.

From morning light to evening's close,
In these moments, our affection grows.
Linked in trust, the ties we weave,
In the book of life, we believe.

Every conflict faced, a lesson learned,
With every turn, our passion burned.
As seasons change, as stories bend,
In the tale of us, there's no end.

So here's to the moments, big and small,
To every rise and even the fall.
In the pages of togetherness we find,
The timeless bond, beautifully defined.

Weaving the Steady Thread

The loom of life, with colors bright,
We twist and turn, through day and night.
In every strand, a vision clear,
We weave our dreams, year to year.

With every knot that ties us close,
Strength in unity, we chose.
Through every challenge, we will see,
A tapestry of you and me.

Softly threading our hopes and fears,
The steady rhythm calms our years.
In patterns rich, our lives unfold,
Stories woven, together told.

As seasons shift and moments fade,
Our fabric sings, it won't degrade.
Each thread a heartbeat, strong and sure,
In this woven bond, we endure.

Forever stitching love's embrace,
In this grand weave, we find our place.
Tangled yet beautiful, life we thread,
Weaving the stories, boldly spread.

The Pulse of Reliability

In every heartbeat, a promise lies,
Trust takes root and never dies.
Through stormy skies and sunlit rays,
Our rhythm stays, through all the ways.

The beat of time, it never stalls,
In silent strength, our courage calls.
Each moment shared, a brick we lay,
In the fortress built, come what may.

With open hearts, we face the days,
A steady pulse that gently sways.
In laughter loud or whispered sighs,
Reliability never lies.

Through thick and thin, we stand as one,
In each heartbeat, our battles won.
Together we breathe, the air so sweet,
The pulse of life, our steady beat.

So here's to us, unwavering, strong,
In life's great symphony, we belong.
Through every trial and joyful tear,
The pulse of reliability, always near.

Unfaltering Beats

In the cadence of our shared life,
Through joy and challenge, love's no strife.
Each moment echoes, loud and clear,
Unfaltering beats, we hold dear.

Steps together, side by side,
In every shift, we softly glide.
With rhythm found in every song,
In perfect harmony, we belong.

Through every rise, through every fall,
In whispered dreams, we hear the call.
With steady hearts, we face the night,
Unfaltering beats, our guiding light.

In every glance, a promise made,
A symphony of love that won't fade.
With hands entwined, we generate,
The music of us, it won't await.

So let's dance on, through thick and thin,
In the heart of life, we find our win.
In synchronicity, we'll roam,
Unfaltering beats, our forever home.

Choreography of Unwavering Bonds

In silence, we sway, hearts intertwined,
A dance of trust, where souls align.
Through every stumble, we find our grace,
Our steps a map, in this sacred space.

With every twirl, our spirits ignite,
In shadows and light, we embrace the night.
Bound by the rhythm, never apart,
Choreography flows from the depth of our heart.

Through storms we glide, steadfast and bold,
A testament to the stories we've told.
In laughter and tears, we weave our song,
In the choreography, where we belong.

With gentle whispers, we share the weight,
In moments of silence, we celebrate fate.
Like waves on the shore, we ebb and flow,
In this dance of life, our love will grow.

Together we rise, like stars that align,
Each step a promise, a bond that shines.
Choreography of unwavering grace,
In each other's arms, we find our place.

The Rhythm of Mutual Support

In the quiet moments, hearts beat as one,
A rhythm of kindness, a race we have run.
With hands held high, we reach for the sky,
In the dance of support, we learn to fly.

Through trials and triumphs, side by side,
Our voices in harmony, we never hide.
In laughter and solace, we find our way,
The rhythm of friendship guides every day.

With gentle nudges, we lift each other,
A bond unyielding, like no other.
In joy and sorrow, together we stand,
The heart's gentle cadence, eternally planned.

When paths are rocky, and shadows grow tall,
In the rhythm of trust, we will never fall.
Steps intertwine, like roots in the ground,
In mutual support, our strength is found.

As the music plays, we dance through the night,
With faith in our hearts, everything feels right.
The rhythm of life, a harmonious tune,
In the embrace of support, we are immune.

Steps of Faithfulness

With every heartbeat, we take a vow,
Steps of faithfulness, here and now.
In whispers of hope, we journey along,
Together we flourish, where we belong.

Through every challenge, our spirits unite,
In the still of the night, we find our light.
With trust as our guide, we bravely proceed,
Steps of faithfulness in every deed.

When doubts creep in, and shadows appear,
In the warmth of our bond, there's nothing to fear.
In patience and kindness, we stitch the seams,
Steps of faithfulness weave our dreams.

In laughter and trials, we dance in the glow,
With steps that echo, together we grow.
Through seasons of change, our promise will last,
Steps of faithfulness, a treasure amassed.

Embracing the journey, hand in hand we stand,
A legacy built on love so grand.
In every heartbeat, our rhythm is true,
Steps of faithfulness, me and you.

The Flow of Assured Companionship

In the gentle embrace of morning light,
We walk together, hearts feeling bright.
The flow of connection, a river so wide,
In the warmth of companionship, we abide.

With every moment that passes by,
We share our dreams, we aim for the sky.
In laughter and comfort, we find our song,
The flow of companionship carries us strong.

Through the trials of life, we'll face the tide,
Assured in our bond, we will never divide.
Hand in hand, like mountains we stand,
The flow of companionship, perfectly planned.

In whispers of hope, our spirits will soar,
Together we journey, always wanting more.
With love as our compass, we navigate deep,
The flow of companionship, a promise to keep.

As seasons will change, we'll dance all the same,
In the warmth of our hearts, we'll fan the flame.
The flow of assured, in each fleeting glance,
Companionship blossoms, a beautiful dance.

Steps of Solace

In a garden where shadows play,
Soft whispers lead the way.
Every step, a gentle sound,
Peace in each movement found.

Beneath the sky, the trees sway,
Nature's calm, here to stay.
With every breath, worries cease,
In solace, I find my peace.

Footprints traced on faded ground,
In this moment, love is found.
Guided by the stars above,
I walk the path, filled with love.

Time slows down, the heart will soar,
With every step, I want more.
Underneath the moonlit glow,
These steps of solace, softly flow.

In the silence, dreams unfurl,
I am free within this world.
Every heartbeat, a silent song,
In this place, I feel I belong.

The Quiet Assurance

In the dawn, a soft embrace,
Quiet moments, sacred space.
Whispers of a gentle breeze,
Lifting spirits, putting hearts at ease.

Calm reflections on the lake,
In stillness, there's no mistake.
Every worry fades away,
Trust in life, come what may.

Facing storms with open hands,
Together, we make our stands.
An unseen strength surrounds us tight,
Giving courage, guiding light.

With every word, a promise made,
In this bond, we are not afraid.
In darkest hours, we find our way,
The quiet assurance here to stay.

Heartbeats sync in perfect time,
Finding joy in simple rhyme.
In unity, we rise above,
Fostering hope, building love.

Unity in Motion

Hands entwined, we start to dance,
In this rhythm, we take a chance.
Together we move, a symphony,
In the flow, we are truly free.

Each step forward, hearts align,
In this moment, your heart is mine.
The world fades as we glide,
With love's power, we won't hide.

Fleeting shadows in the night,
Together we chase the light.
With every turn, we grow and learn,
In motion, the fire will burn.

Through every twist, through every bend,
Our spirit soars, no need to pretend.
In this dance, a bond so strong,
In unity, we all belong.

The music swells, our hearts will soar,
In this embrace, we crave for more.
Discount the doubt, let love be seen,
Unity in motion, pure and keen.

Rhythm of Reassurance

In the silence, hear the beat,
A melody, so pure, so sweet.
Every pulse, a soothing sound,
In this rhythm, hope is found.

Softly stepping through the night,
Guided by the stars so bright.
In the dark, we find our way,
In the music, come what may.

Echoes of the heart arise,
Through the storms, we touch the skies.
Every note, a gentle sign,
In this dance, our spirits shine.

Together we sing, hand in hand,
Creating dreams, a wonderland.
In every phrase, reassurance flows,
With each heartbeat, love just grows.

In the twilight, as shadows play,
Feel the rhythm guide the way.
Together, we embrace the night,
In the dark, we find the light.

Eternal Dance of Interdependence

In the shadows, we find our light,
Every step, a shared delight.
Hands entwined as we sway and spin,
Together, we lose, together we win.

Whispers of love fill the air,
A gentle bond that we both share.
Each heartbeat a promise, a timeless song,
In this dance, we both belong.

Moments fleeting, yet they persist,
In sync, we flow, none can resist.
With every twirl, a world unfolds,
Our stories intertwine like threads of gold.

Through challenges fierce, we stand tall,
With you beside me, we shall not fall.
A tapestry woven with trust and grace,
In this dance of life, we find our place.

In the silence, I feel your breath,
A sacred bond that conquers death.
In this eternal waltz, we stride,
Side by side, forever allied.

The Atlas of Mutual Support

Upon your shoulders, I find my way,
Your strength, my guide, come what may.
Together we map the vast unknown,
In this journey, we have grown.

With every word, a bridge we build,
In the quiet, our hearts are filled.
You give me courage, I lend my hand,
In this life, together we stand.

Through trials and storms, we face it all,
In every rise, we never stall.
Your voice, a beacon, lighting the night,
In shared dreams, we ignite our flight.

Boundless the paths our spirits roam,
In your embrace, I've found my home.
A map of love, our guiding star,
Together, we'll always go far.

With every step, our trust expands,
In unity, we make our plans.
Through valleys low and peaks that soar,
This atlas of support, forevermore.

Glistening Threads of Faithful Ties

In the fabric of life, we weave our seams,
Threads of trust, woven with dreams.
With every knot, a promise made,
In every stitch, our fears allayed.

These glistening ties bind us near,
In every whisper, I hold you dear.
Together we face what life imparts,
With these faithful threads, united hearts.

Through shadows cast and moments bright,
In every challenge, we find the light.
Interwoven paths, a sacred art,
With every strand, you touch my heart.

In laughter's echo, in sorrow's sigh,
These threads endure, they never lie.
For in our bond, the world we see,
A tapestry of you and me.

With gentle hands, we craft our tale,
In woven whispers, we shall prevail.
The fabric of love, a vibrant hue,
Glistening threads, forever true.

Boundless Horizons of Trust

Upon the horizon, dreams arise,
Beneath the vast, embracing skies.
Hand in hand, we chase the dawn,
In this journey, we carry on.

With trust as our compass, we find our way,
Through every night, into the day.
In every glance, possibilities bloom,
Together, we conquer every room.

With every story, a new world starts,
In shared adventures, we play our parts.
With open hearts, we greet the sun,
In boundless horizons, we become one.

Through valleys deep and mountains high,
The strength of trust lifts us to the sky.
Hand in hand, we rise above,
In every challenge, we find our love.

And as we wander, let it be known,
In every moment, we have grown.
With every heartbeat, a promise we keep,
In boundless trust, we soar and leap.

Synchronized Strokes of Support

In the calm of the morning light,
We stand together, ready to fight.
Each heartbeat a rhythm, strong and true,
In this dance of life, it's me and you.

Shoulders joined, we rise and fall,
In moments of doubt, we hear the call.
Hands entwined, we share the load,
Together we walk, we've found our road.

With every step, our spirits blend,
In an endless journey, we shall not bend.
Through storms and waves, we'll weather it all,
In the synergy of love, we stand tall.

Trust in each other, our guiding star,
No distance too great, no challenge too far.
As tides shift and time flows,
We'll be the anchor, that's how it goes.

Bound by the promise, forever we'll strive,
In this mighty current, we come alive.
Through synchronized strokes, our spirits unite,
Together in harmony, we ignite.

The Waltz of Unbreakable Ties

In the silence, our shadows sway,
With each twirl, we seize the day.
A bond that's forged, so pure and bright,
In this waltz of love, we find our light.

Step by step, we move as one,
With every glance, our journey's begun.
Echoes of laughter fill the air,
In this dance, there's magic to share.

Through every stumble, we'll find our pace,
In the warmth of your arms, I'll find my place.
Together we glide, through joys and fears,
In the rhythm of trust, we lose our tears.

The music swells, a tender embrace,
In unison, we conquer time and space.
With every turn, the world fades away,
In this waltz of hearts, forever we'll stay.

As the night unfolds, we'll dance till dawn,
In the glow of love, our spirits are drawn.
Through unbreakable ties, we'll find our way,
In this sacred dance, we're here to stay.

Pathways of Faith and Loyalty

On winding roads, our steps align,
In every heartbeat, a sign divine.
With faith as our guide, we'll journey far,
Together we're stronger, that's who we are.

Through thickets and thorn, we find the light,
With loyalty's torch, we vanquish the night.
As we wander through valleys, hand in hand,
In unity's power, we boldly stand.

With every dawn, our spirits rise,
Seeking new wonders beneath the skies.
In laughter and tears, we share the way,
Our hearts intertwined, come what may.

Through trials and peaks, we'll share our dreams,
On this path of faith, with radiant beams.
As storms may challenge, we won't lose sight,
Our bond is eternal, through day and night.

In the tapestry woven of moments shared,
With love as our compass, we are prepared.
Pathways of faith, where loyalties shine,
Together we'll flourish, your hand in mine.

Chorus of Shared Promises

In the stillness, our voices rise,
A chorus of dreams beneath the skies.
With each promise, a seed we sow,
Together we flourish, together we grow.

In whispers of comfort, we find our song,
With melodies sweet, we can't go wrong.
Every vow a note, every glance a beat,
In harmony's embrace, our hearts will meet.

Through shadows and light, we weave our thread,
In laughter and joy, love's whispers spread.
With every heartbeat, our anthem rings,
In the bond that we share, our spirit sings.

As seasons change, our tune stays true,
In the dance of the world, it's me and you.
With hands clasped tightly, we'll face the storm,
In the warmth of our promises, we'll transform.

In the symphony of life, we share our grace,
With each breath, we cherish this space.
A chorus of shared promises, bold and bright,
Together we shine, in love's pure light.

Pavilion of Assurance

Underneath the sturdy dome,
Whispers of hope gently roam.
Soft light dances on the floor,
Every heart feels safe and sure.

Woven dreams in every seam,
Carried forth like a warm beam.
Together, fears drift away,
In this space, we choose to stay.

Fields of peace stretch far and wide,
Side by side, we choose our guide.
Trust and love in every breath,
Here within, we conquer death.

Gentle hands entwined so tight,
Our shadows blend in soft twilight.
Stories shared beneath the stars,
In this place, we bear no scars.

In the hush, we find our way,
Each promise spoken, here to stay.
Trust builds bridges from our hearts,
Together, never be apart.

Unfolding Trust in Quiet Moments

In the silence, eyes meet eyes,
Comfort blooms without disguise.
Fingers brush, the world stands still,
In this pause, we taste the thrill.

Time a river, flowing slow,
Anchored by the trust we know.
Every murmur, every sigh,
Lifts our spirits, lets them fly.

Moments linger, softly shared,
In this haven, love declared.
Gentle laughter, warm embrace,
Close enough to feel the grace.

Through the shadows, truth reveals,
In each heartbeat, love appeals.
Quiet whispers weave a thread,
Binding souls, where hope is fed.

Trust unfolds, a tapestry,
Painted bright, yet bittersweet.
In your eyes, I see the light,
Together, we embrace the night.

The Steady Heartbeat of Companionship

Side by side, we walk the lane,
In the sun and in the rain.
Every heartbeat, strong and true,
This rhythm binds me close to you.

In our laughter, joy takes flight,
Through the dark, we find the light.
Fingers laced, a sacred trust,
In companionship, we must.

Silent moments, shared with grace,
Each heartbeat finds its own place.
Counting blessings, one, two, three,
Two hearts join in harmony.

Journeys made, both far and near,
In your presence, I feel clear.
Storms may come, but here we stand,
Heart to heart, hand in hand.

Together, we write our tale,
On the winds, we set our sail.
In every chapter, love will guide,
The steady heartbeat by our side.

Trail of Faithful Shadows

Beneath the trees, our shadows play,
Guiding us along the way.
Footprints left on paths of trust,
In the quiet, hope is thrust.

With every step, we weave a bond,
In the light, we grow fond.
Whispers echo through the night,
In our hearts, we find the light.

The trail unfolds, a sacred space,
Hand in hand, we set the pace.
Every turn a new embrace,
Together, we find our place.

Through the shadows, faith we chase,
In your eyes, I see my grace.
With every heartbeat, come what may,
I'll follow you along this way.

As the stars begin to gleam,
We wander, lost in a dream.
In this journey, we shall find,
Love eternal, intertwined.

The Beat of Lifelong Allies

Through laughter and tears, we stand strong,
In shadows and light, where we belong.
A bond forged in trust, through stormy skies,
Together we rise, no need for disguise.

Memories crafted with each fleeting day,
We cherish the moments, come what may.
With whispers of hope, we face the night,
Our hearts beat as one, a powerful sight.

In silence we speak, in comfort we find,
The strength to move forward, our spirits aligned.
Side by side in the dance of years,
We conquer our worries, dissolve all fears.

Through valleys of doubt and mountains of strife,
Our spirits entwined, the essence of life.
In laughter and sorrow, through thick and through thin,
Together forever, let the journey begin.

With every heartbeat, our spirits entwine,
Lifelong allies, a bond so divine.
In the tapestry woven, our stories unite,
In the beat of our hearts, we ignite the light.

Fluttering Attachments

Like petals on wind, we flutter and sway,
In fields of affection, we find our way.
With whispers of joy and laughter so sweet,
Each moment together, a delicate treat.

In sunlight's embrace, we linger and play,
Creating connections that never decay.
The dance of our spirits, so vibrant, alive,
In the warmth of our friendship, we truly thrive.

Through seasons of change, we gracefully shift,
Each flutter a sign of the love we uplift.
The echoes of kindness, our hearts gently trace,
In the garden of life, we blossom with grace.

As shadows may loom, and tempests may rise,
We weather the storms, look towards the skies.
With fluttering hearts, we nurture and care,
In the fabric of friendship, a bond we declare.

In moments of stillness, in chaos's call,
We stand intertwined, strong through it all.
With fluttering attachments, in rhythm we soar,
Together forever, we seek to explore.

Cadence of Constant Care

In gentle rhythms, our hearts find a song,
A cadence of care that helps us belong.
Each gesture a note, in life's wondrous play,
We nurture the bond, let worries decay.

With open arms, we embrace the delight,
In the warmth of our shelter, the world feels right.
Through whispers of comfort, we gather our strength,
Uniting our journeys, with measures and length.

In laughter's bright echoes, and tears that we share,
We weave a sweet tapestry, woven with care.
Our spirits in harmony, lifting us high,
In the cadence of love, we learn how to fly.

On paths intertwined, through each shifting scene,
We celebrate triumphs, and dream what we mean.
In the cadence of constant, unyielding embrace,
We flourish together, our hearts find their place.

With every heartbeat, we nurture the dance,
In the rhythm of friendship, we take our chance.
Through the cadence of life, forever we tread,
With constant care guiding where hopes are fed.

Unfurling the Fabric of Dependability

In the weft and the weave, our stories unfold,
A fabric of trust, in threads bright and bold.
With each loyal stitch, our bond tightly sewn,
In the heart of the storm, we never feel alone.

Through colors of laughter, and shades of our pain,
We hold one another in sunshine and rain.
Each moment a fiber, each memory a seam,
In the fabric of life, we follow the dream.

Against all the odds, together we stand,
In the strength of our union, we lend a hand.
With patterns of kindness, we build and create,
A tapestry rich, our shared love innate.

Through seasons of trial and joys that we share,
We toughen the fibers with infinite care.
In unfurling layers, revealing our heart,
In the fabric of dependability, we never part.

With threads woven tightly, we stand side by side,
In the warmth of our bond, we will always abide.
In this fabric of life, through thick and through thin,
Dependable hearts reflect the love within.

Interlaced Destinies

In the weave of stars so bright,
Two souls dance in soft twilight.
Fate entwines with gentle grace,
Guiding hearts to a shared place.

Whispers of dreams entwined as one,
Under the canvas of the sun.
Paths converge, a sacred thread,
In every step, love is spread.

Through trials faced, they find their way,
In laughter shared and hopes at bay.
Invisible hands, they both hold tight,
Interlaced destinies, pure delight.

Across the seas, their spirits soar,
A bond unbroken, forevermore.
With every heartbeat, the story grows,
In the tapestry, love forever flows.

As seasons change, their roots run deep,
With memories cherished, they safely keep.
In the fabric of life, a gentle tease,
Interlaced destinies, hearts at ease.

A Tangle of Hearts United

In the garden where laughter gleams,
A tangle of hearts weave together dreams.
Colors blend in a fragrant air,
United by love, a bond so rare.

Hand in hand through the evening glow,
With whispered secrets, their feelings flow.
Each moment cherished, every glance adored,
In their hearts, a truth restored.

As shadows fade, the night unfolds,
A story of warmth and joy retold.
With every heartbeat, they find their way,
In this dance of love, forever they'll stay.

Through storms and trials, they face the tide,
In unity strong, they will abide.
Knotted together, their fates align,
A tangle of hearts, beautifully entwined.

With laughter and tears, a journey shared,
In every challenge, they have dared.
Together they flourish, side by side,
In each other's arms, they'll always reside.

The Embrace of Familiar Footprints

In the sand where memories lie,
Familiar footprints, a sweet goodbye.
Tracing paths of love and grace,
Where every step finds its place.

With gentle waves that kiss the shore,
Echoes of laughter linger evermore.
In the hush of dusk, they softly meet,
An embrace of warmth, oh so sweet.

Through seasons passed, they make their mark,
In the stories shared beneath the dark.
Each footprint tells a tale so dear,
The embrace of love that conquers fear.

As stars arise and shadows play,
Those footprints guide them on their way.
In every heartbeat, a tender call,
The embrace of familiar stands tall.

Time may shift, but love stays true,
In footsteps woven, a bond renew.
Through every journey, come what may,
The embrace of love shall lead the way.

Crescent Moons of Confidence

In twilight's glow, a crescent beam,
Whispers of hope begin to dream.
With every phase, their spirits rise,
Beneath the moonlit, open skies.

In shadows cast, they find their light,
Crescent moons guide hearts to flight.
With courage born from starlit grace,
They chase their dreams, each challenge faced.

Through valleys low and mountains high,
Confidence blooms, like stars on high.
In every heartbeat, they hear the call,
To embrace their truth and stand up tall.

Beneath the sky, where wishes sing,
The moon brings strength, a gentle wing.
With every cycle, they learn and grow,
Crescent moons teach them how to flow.

In the night's embrace, they find their ground,
Confidence reigns, love unbound.
With each new phase, hearts realign,
Crescent moons of confidence, truly divine.

Radiating Dependability in the Dark

In shadows deep, a light does shine,
A steady flame, a bond divine.
Through trials faced, we stand as one,
Together bright, till night is done.

In whispered fears, your hand I find,
A silent strength, our hearts aligned.
In darkest hours, your warmth stays near,
A guiding star, dispelling fear.

With every tear that falls like rain,
We share the weight of shared disdain.
Yet rise again, like dawn's embrace,
Resilient souls, in time and space.

In trust we build, a fortress strong,
A safe retreat where we belong.
With steady hearts, we face the night,
In unity, we find our light.

The Emblem of Unfaltering Hearts

In every glance, a promise lies,
A glance of hope beneath the skies.
With open arms, we hold the flame,
A bond that time cannot disclaim.

In moments shared, we find our way,
With every word, in love we play.
An emblem forged of laughter's sound,
In you, my love, my heart is bound.

Through tempest wild, we sail as one,
In unison, our hearts have won.
With steadfast gaze, we journey on,
Together strong, till fears are gone.

In gentle whispers, secrets shared,
Our tapestry of trust declared.
With each heartbeat, we intertwine,
Your soul with mine, forever mine.

Fluid Movements of Harmonious Bonds

In graceful dance, our spirits meet,
A rhythm found in heartbeat's beat.
With every step, a story spun,
In fluid grace, our lives are one.

Through changing tides, we sway and flow,
In mirrored movements, love will grow.
With open hearts, we navigate,
The course of life, we celebrate.

With laughter's song, our souls take flight,
In joyous harmony, pure delight.
With gentle hands, we trace the line,
Of memories made, our love divine.

As seasons shift, our bond remains,
Through joy and pain, the love sustains.
In every turn, our spirits blend,
In fluid harmony, love won't end.

Mapping Out Lifeline Threads

With every thread, a story weaves,
In vibrant colors, love believes.
A tapestry of dreams unfolds,
With whispered hopes, our journey told.

Through valleys low and mountains high,
We trace the paths where hearts can fly.
Each moment shared, a stitch so fine,
In every heartbeat, our lives align.

In tangled knots, we find our way,
A dance of fate, come what may.
Together threaded by love's design,
A lifeline spun, forever entwined.

With guiding stars, we chart the course,
A journey fueled by love's pure force.
In every twist, our souls will glide,
Through time and space, forever tied.

Sheltering Shadows

In the quiet grove we stand,
Under branches, hand in hand.
Whispers of the leaves above,
Embrace the warmth of endless love.

Sunset paints the sky with gold,
Ancient stories softly told.
Guardians of our dreams so bright,
In shadows, we find our light.

Through the night, the stars will gleam,
Guiding us through every dream.
In the silence, hearts entwine,
Forever yours, forever mine.

Time may fade, but we will stay,
Bound by love, come what may.
In the beauty of this land,
Sheltering shadows, side by side we stand.

With each dawn, we start anew,
In the light, our love shines through.
Together here, we slowly grow,
In the warmth of shadows' glow.

Dance of Loyalty

In the moonlight, we take flight,
Two souls moving, hearts alight.
With every step, the world fades,
In this moment, love cascades.

Through trials faced, we stand so tall,
In our rhythm, we won't fall.
Each promise made, a sacred vow,
In the dance of now, here and how.

When storms arise, we'll anchor fast,
Holding tight, our love will last.
Through every twist, each turn we make,
In loyalty, no hearts will break.

As seasons change, our song endures,
In each heartbeat, our love assures.
Together in this timeless trance,
We'll always find our way to dance.

With every glance, a spark ignites,
In the silence, we share our sights.
Bound by trust, our spirits fly,
In this dance, we touch the sky.

The Unbroken Circle

In a world that spins so fast,
We hold onto the moments passed.
Through the years, our laughter sings,
In the circle, love brings wings.

Every glance, a story told,
In our hearts, we find the gold.
Together, hand in hand we stand,
The unbroken thread, heart's command.

Memories weave like threads of light,
Binding us through day and night.
In the tapestry we create,
Love is woven, never late.

When paths diverge, we'll find the way,
With every dawn, a new display.
In the circle, we know no end,
Through every turn, we still transcend.

With every beat, our hearts align,
In love's embrace, forever shine.
Together we rise, never apart,
In the unbroken circle of the heart.

Cadence of Companionship

In the meadow, hand in hand,
Together, we boldly stand.
With laughter woven through the air,
In each moment, love declared.

Walking paths both old and new,
Every step, I'm close to you.
In the rhythm of our song,
Finding where we both belong.

Through the trials, side by side,
In your gaze, I take my ride.
With every heartbeat, we will sway,
In the cadence of the day.

When the winds begin to howl,
I will always hear your soul.
Like the stars that light the dark,
You ignite the endless spark.

With every sunrise, I am blessed,
In your arms, I find my rest.
Together, we will face the storm,
In companionship, our hearts keep warm.

Patterns of Faith

In the quiet of the morning light,
Whispers of hope soar to new heights.
Each heartbeat echoes a promise made,
In the tapestry of dreams, we're laid.

Threads of love entwine and bind,
Carving paths through the heart and mind.
With every step, a journey unfolds,
The stories of courage, forever told.

Through storms we stand, together strong,
Each note of faith, a sacred song.
In shadows deep, the light still glows,
Guiding our way, wherever it flows.

In moments of doubt, we seek the truth,
In laughter and tears, we find our youth.
Through valleys low and mountains high,
Our spirits rise, reaching for the sky.

In every heartbeat, a pattern of grace,
In every prayer, we find our place.
Together we weave, fierce and bold,
Patterns of faith, as life unfolds.

Sway of Sincerity

Beneath the oak, where shadows play,
We dance to the rhythm, come what may.
In the sway of leaves, truth is found,
A gentle embrace, all around.

Words unsaid, yet hearts collide,
In the silence, love won't hide.
Every glance speaks what we hold,
Stories shared, brave and bold.

In the laughter that lifts the day,
In the tears that softly stray,
We carve a path of honesty,
In the strength of our sincerity.

As seasons change, our roots run deep,
In trust we gather, in love we keep.
Each moment a thread, woven tight,
In the colors of day and night.

Through the dance of time and space,
The sway of sincerity holds its grace.
Together we move, heart in hand,
In the light of truth, we forever stand.

The Unseen Hand

In the quiet hour before the dawn,
A gentle touch, unseen yet drawn.
Guiding us softly, like the breeze,
Through the trials, it brings us ease.

With every choice, a path appears,
Woven with hopes, laced with fears.
Yet, in the chaos, a calm does land,
A whisper of peace, the unseen hand.

In moments of doubt, we feel the push,
A nudge of courage, in every hush.
Through winding roads and shifting sands,
We navigate life, held by unseen hands.

As stars align in the velvet night,
Wonders unfold, hidden from sight.
We turn our gaze to the greater plan,
Finding solace in the unseen hand.

Binding us close, a cosmic dance,
In the mystery of fate, we find our chance.
Together we journey, forever grand,
Embraced by the warmth of the unseen hand.

Balanced Together

On the line between night and day,
We find the truth, come what may.
In the ebb and flow, we learn to thrive,
In the harmony, we come alive.

With hearts aligned, we share the weight,
In the dance of life, we celebrate.
Through highs and lows, the world spins round,
In balance together, true love is found.

In laughter we rise, in silence we ground,
In the cadence of life, a beautiful sound.
We lift each other, like the sun in flight,
In the colors of dusk, we shine so bright.

Through storms we weather, hand in hand,
In the gift of moments, we take a stand.
In every heartbeat, a rhythm we share,
Balanced together, we conquer despair.

As seasons change, our bond remains,
In the dance of love, joy sustains.
United as one, we journey forth,
In the balance of life, we find our worth.

Milton Keynes UK
Ingram Content Group UK Ltd.
UKHW022049111124
451035UK00014B/1019